# As A Man Thinketh

James Allen

# As a Man Thinketh

Edited for Contemporary Readers
by William R. Webb

Illustrated by
James Hamil

HALLMARK EDITIONS

# CONTENTS

# As A Man Thinketh

"We become spiritually rich when we discover the adventure within; when we are conscious of the oneness of all life; when we experience kinship with nature; when we know the power of meditation."

# WHO WAS JAMES ALLEN?

JAMES ALLEN is a literary mystery man. His inspirational classic, *As A Man Thinketh,* has influenced millions for good. Yet today he remains almost unknown.

None of his nineteen books gives a clue to his life other than to mention his place of residence — Ilfracombe, England. His name cannot be found in a major reference work. Not even the Library of Congress or the British Museum has much to say about him.

Who was this man who believed in the power of thought to bring fame, fortune and happiness? Was he able to help others, but not himself? Or did he, as Henry David Thoreau says, "hear a different drummer"?

James Allen never gained fame or fortune. That much is true. His was a quiet, unrewarded genius. He seldom made enough money from his writings to cover expenses. He did not bother to copyright his books outside England, apparently preferring to leave them in the public domain. One fortunate result of this preference is that *As A Man Thinketh* has been widely published.

Allen was born in Leicester, Central England, November 28, 1864. The family business failed within a few years and in 1879 his father left for America in an effort to recoup his losses. The elder Allen had hoped to settle in the United States, but was robbed and murdered before he could send for his family.

The financial crisis that resulted forced James to leave school at fifteen. He eventually became a private secretary, a position that would be called "administrative assistant" today. He worked in this capacity for several British manufacturers until 1902, when he decided to devote all his time to writing.

Unfortunately, Allen's literary career was short, lasting only nine years, until his death in 1912. During that period he wrote nineteen books, a rich outpouring of ideas that have lived on to inspire later generations.

Soon after finishing his first book, *From Poverty To Power,* Allen moved to Ilfracombe, on England's southwest coast. The little resort town with its seafront Victorian hotels and its rolling hills and winding lanes offered him the quiet atmosphere he needed to pursue his philosophical studies.

*As A Man Thinketh* was Allen's second book. Despite its subsequent popularity he was dissatisfied with it. Even though it was his most concise and eloquent work, the book that best embodied his thought, he somehow failed to recognize its value. His wife Lily had to persuade him to publish it.

James Allen strove to live the ideal life described by Russia's great novelist and mystic Count Leo Tolstoy—the life of voluntary poverty, manual labor and ascetic self-discipline. Like Tolstoy, Allen sought to improve himself, be happy, and master all of the virtues. His search for "felicity for man on earth" was typically Tolstoyan.

According to his wife, Allen "wrote when he had a message, and it became a message only when he had lived it in his own life, and knew that it was good."

His day in Ilfracombe began with a predawn walk up to the Cairn, a stony spot on the hillside overlooking his home and the sea. He would remain there for an hour in meditation. Then he would return to the house and spend the morning writing. The afternoons were devoted to gardening, a pastime he enjoyed. His evenings were spent in conversation with those who were interested in his work.

A friend described Allen as "a frail-looking little man, Christlike, with a mass of flowing black hair."

"I think of him especially in the black velvet suit he always wore in the evenings," the friend wrote. "He would talk quietly to a small group of us then—English, French, Austrian and Indian—of meditation, of philosophy, of Tolstoy or Buddha, and of killing nothing, not even a mouse in the garden.

"He overawed us all a little because of his appearance, his gentle conversation, and especially because he went out to commune with God on the hills before dawn."

James Allen's philosophy became possible when liberal Protestantism discarded the stern dogma that man is sinful by nature. It substituted for that dogma an optimistic belief in man's innate goodness and divine rationality.

This reversal of doctrine was, as William James said, the greatest revolution of the 19th Century. It was part of a move toward a reconciliation between science and religion following Darwin's publication of *The Origin of Species*.

Charles Darwin, himself, hinted at the change in belief in *The Descent of Man*. In that book he wrote, "the highest possible stage in moral culture is when we recognize that we ought to control our thoughts."

Allen's work embodies the influence of Protestant liberalism on the one hand and of Buddhist thought on the other. For example, the Buddha teaches, "All that we are is the result of what we have thought." Allen's Biblical text says, "As a man thinketh in his heart, so is he."

Allen insists upon the power of the individual to form his own character and to create his own happiness. "Thought and character are one," he says, "and as character can only manifest and discover itself through environment and circumstance, the outer conditions of a person's life will always be found to be harmoniously related to his inner state. This does not mean that a man's circumstances at any given time are an indication of his entire character, but that those circumstances are so intimately connected with some vital thought element within him that, for the time being, they are indispensable to his development."

Allen starts us thinking—even when we would rather be doing something else. He tells us how thought leads to action. He shows us how to turn our dreams into realities.

His is a philosophy that has brought success to millions. It is the philosophy of Norman Vincent Peale's *The Power of Positive Thinking* and of Joshua Liebman's *Peace of Mind*.

We become spiritually rich, Allen writes, when we discover the adventure within; when we are conscious of the oneness of all life; when we know the power of meditation; when we experience kinship with nature.

Allen's message is one of hope even in the midst of confusion. "Yes," he says, "humanity surges with uncontrolled passion, is tumultuous with ungoverned grief, is blown about by anxiety and doubt. Only the wise man, only he whose thoughts are controlled and purified, makes the winds and the storms of the soul obey him."

"Tempest-tossed souls," Allen continues, "wherever you may be, under whatsoever conditions you may live, know this—in the ocean of life the isles of blessedness are smiling and the sunny shore of your ideal awaits your coming. . . ."

And thus Allen teaches two essential truths: today we are where our thoughts have taken us, and we are the architects—for better or worse—of our futures.

# Selected Writings

"Act is the blossom of theory and joy
and suffering are its fruits..."

# Thought and Character

*Whatsoever things are true, whatsoever things are honest, whatsoever things are just, whatsoever things are pure, whatsoever things are lovely, whatsoever things are of good report: . . . . think on these things.*   PHILIPPIANS 4:8

THE APHORISM, "As a man thinketh in his heart, so is he," embraces the whole of a man's being. It is so comprehensive that it reaches out to every condition and circumstance of life. A man is literally what he thinks. His character is the sum of all his thoughts.

As the plant springs from the seed, and could not be without it, so every act of a man springs from the hidden seeds of thought. This truth applies as equally to those acts called "spontaneous" as to those which are deliberate.

Act is the blossom of thought, and joy and suffering are its fruits; thus a man harvests the sweet and bitter fruits of his own husbandry.

Man is a growth by law, and not a creation by artifice, for cause and effect is as absolute and undeviating in the hidden realm of thought as in the world of visible and material things.

A noble character is not a thing of favor or chance, but the natural result of continued effort in right thinking, the effect of long-cherished association with noble thoughts. An ignoble and bestial character, by the same process, is the result of the continued harboring of sensual thoughts.

### YOUR FATE IS IN YOUR HANDS

Man is made or unmade by himself. In the armory of thought he forges the weapons by which he destroys himself. He also fashions the tools with which he builds for himself heavenly mansions of joy and strength and peace. By the right choice and true application of thought, man ascends to divine perfection. By the abuse and wrong application of thought, he descends below the level of the beast. Between these two are all the grades of character, and man is their maker and master.

Of all the beautiful truths pertaining to the soul, none is more gladdening or fruitful of divine promise and confidence than this — that man is the master of thought, the molder of character, and the maker and shaper of condition, environment, and destiny.

### MAN THE MASTER

As a being of power, intelligence, and love, and the lord of his own thoughts, man holds the key to every situation, and has within himself the means of transforming himself into what he wills.

Man is always the master. Even in his weakness and degradation he is the foolish master who misgoverns his "household." When he begins to reflect upon his condition, and to search diligently for the law upon which his being is established, he becomes the wise master. He then begins directing his energies with intelligence, and fashioning his thoughts toward a fruitful life.

Such is the conscious master, and man can only master himself by discovering within himself the laws of thought, a discovery which is totally a matter of application, self-analysis, and experience.

### TRUTH LIES WITHIN YOU

Only by searching and mining are gold and diamonds obtained, and, similarly, man can find every truth connected with his being if he will dig deep into the mine of his soul.

Man is the maker of his character, the molder of his life, and the builder of his destiny. This he may prove unerringly, if he will watch, control, and alter his thoughts, tracing their effects upon himself, upon others, and upon his life and circumstances. This he may prove, if he will link cause and effect by patient practice and investigation, and utilize his every experience, even to the most trivial, everyday occurrence, as a means of obtaining that knowledge of himself which is understanding, wisdom, power.

In this direction, as in no other, is the law absolute that "He that seeketh findeth; and to him that knocketh it shall be opened." For only by patience, practice, and ceaseless pursuit can a man enter the door of the temple of knowledge.

"A man's mind is like a garden
which may be cultivated or allowed
to run wild."

# Revealing Your Inner Nature

*It is the mind that maketh good or ill,*
*That maketh wretch or happy, rich or*
*poor.*　　　　EDMUND SPENSER

A MAN'S mind is like a garden, which may be intelligently cultivated or allowed to run wild. But whether cultivated or neglected, it must, and will, bring forth. If no useful seeds are put into it, then an abundance of useless weed seeds will fall into it, and will continue to produce their useless kind.

Just as a gardener cultivates his plot, keeping it free from weeds, and grows the flowers and fruits which he needs, so may a man tend the garden of his mind, weeding out all the wrong, useless, and impure thoughts, and cultivating all the right, useful, and pure thoughts. By this process, a man sooner or later discovers that he is the master gardener of his soul, the director of his life.

He also reveals, within himself, the laws of thought, and understands, with ever-increasing accuracy, how thought forces and mind elements operate in shaping his character, circumstances, and destiny.

Thought and character are one, and as character can only manifest and discover itself through environment and circumstance, the outer conditions of a person's life will always be found to be harmoniously related to his inner state. This does not mean that a man's circumstances at any given time are an indication of his entire character, but that those circumstances are so intimately connected with some vital thought element within him that, for the time being, they are indispensable to his development.

Every man is where he is by the law of his being. The thoughts which he has built into his character have brought him there, and in the arrangement of his life there is no element of chance. All is the result of a law which cannot err. This is just as true of those who feel "out of harmony" with their surroundings as of those who are contented with them.

### THE ROLE OF CIRCUMSTANCE

As a progressive and evolving being, man is where he is that he may learn that he may grow. And as he learns the spiritual lesson which individual circumstance hold for him, they pass away and give way to others.

Man is buffeted by circumstances so long as he believes himself to be the pawn of outside conditions. But when he realizes that he is a creative power, and that he may command the hidden soil and seeds of his being out of which circumstances grow, he then becomes his own master.

Every man who has for any length of time practiced self-control and self-purification knows that circumstances grow out of thought. He will have noticed that the alteration in his circumstances has been in an exact ratio with his altered mental condition. So true is this that when a man earnestly applies himself to remedy the defects in his character, and makes swift and marked progress, he passes rapidly through a succession of changes.

The soul attracts that which it secretly harbors; that which it loves, and also that which it fears. The soul reaches the height of its cherished aspirations; it falls to the level of its unchastened desires —and circumstances are the means by which it receives its own.

Every thought-seed sown or allowed to fall into the mind, and to take root there, produces its own, blossoming sooner or later into act, and bearing its own fruit of opportunity and circumstance. Good thoughts bear good fruit, bad thoughts bad.

The outer world of circumstance shapes itself to the inner world of thought, and both pleasant and unpleasant external conditions are factors which make for the ultimate good of the individual. As the reaper of his own harvest, man learns from both suffering and happiness.

By following his inmost desires, aspirations, and thoughts (pursuing the will-o'-the-wisps of impure imaginings or steadfastly walking the highway of strong and high endeavor), a man is at last fulfilled in the outer conditions of his life.

### YOUR TRUE SELF REVEALED

A man does not come to poverty or go to jail through the tyranny of fate or circumstance, but by the pathway of base thoughts and desires. Nor does a pure-minded man suddenly fall into crime by stress of external force. The criminal thought had long been secretly fostered in his heart, and the hour of his sin revealed its gathered power. Circumstance does not make the man; it reveals him to himself. No such conditions can exist in a man as vice and its attendant sufferings apart from vicious inclinations, or virtue and its pure happiness without the continued cultivation of virtuous aspirations.

Man, therefore, as the lord and master of thought, is the maker of himself, the shaper and author of environment. Even at birth the soul comes to its own. And through every step of its earthly pilgrimage it attracts those combinations of conditions which reveal itself, which are the reflections of its own purity and impurity, its strength and weakness.

Men do not attract that which they want, but that which they are. Their whims, fancies, and ambitions are thwarted at every step, but their inmost thoughts and desires are fed with their own food, be it foul or clean. The "divinity that shapes our ends" is in ourselves; it is our very self. Man is manacled only by himself. Thought and action are the jailers of fate—they imprison, being base; they are also the angels of freedom— they liberate, being noble.

A man does not get what he wishes and prays for, but what he justly earns. His wishes and prayers are only gratified and answered when they harmonize with his thoughts and actions.

In the light of truth, what then is the meaning of "fighting against circumstances"? It means that a man is continually revolting against an effect without, while all the time he is nourishing and preserving its cause in his heart. That cause may take the form of a conscious vice or an unconscious weakness; but whatever it is, it stubbornly retards the efforts of its possessor, and calls for remedy.

Men are anxious to improve their circumstances, but are unwilling to improve themselves; they therefore remain bound. The man who shrinks from self-crucifixion can never accomplish the object upon which his heart is set. This is as true of earthly as of heavenly things. Even the man whose sole object is to acquire wealth must be prepared to make great personal sacrifices before he can accomplish his object. How much more must he sacrifice who would live a strong and well-poised life?

Here is a man who is wretchedly poor. He is extremely anxious to improve his surroundings and home comforts. Yet he continually shirks his work, and feels he is justified in trying to deceive his employer because of the insufficiency of his wages. Such a man does not understand the simplest principles of true prosperity. He is not only totally unfitted to rise out of his wretchedness, but is actually attracting to himself a still deeper wretchedness by dwelling in, and acting out, indolent, deceptive, and unmanly thoughts.

Here is a rich man who is the victim of a painful and persistent disease as the result of gluttony. He is willing to give large sums of money to get rid of it, but he will not sacrifice his gluttonous desires. He wants to gratify his taste for rich foods and have his health as well. Such a man has no chance of regaining his health, because he has not yet learned the first principles of a healthy life.

Here is an employer who adopts crooked measures to avoid paying regulation wages, and, in the hope of increasing profits, reduces the wages of his workers. Such a man is altogether unfitted for prosperity, and when he finds himself bankrupt, both in reputation and riches, he blames circumstances, not knowing that he is the sole author of his condition.

I have introduced these three cases merely to illustrate the truth that man is the cause (though usually unconsciously) of circumstances, and that, while aiming at a good end, he is continually frustrating its accomplishment by encouraging thoughts and desires which cannot possibly harmonize with that end. Such cases could be multiplied and varied almost indefinitely, but mere external facts cannot serve as a ground of reasoning.

### THE VEIL BETWEEN US

Circumstances are so complicated, thought is so deeply rooted, and the conditions of happiness vary so vastly with individuals, that a man's entire soul condition (although it may be known to himself) cannot be judged by another. A man may be honest in certain directions, yet suffer privations;

as a man may be dishonest in certain directions, yet acquire wealth.

But the conclusion usually formed that one man fails because of his particular honesty, and another prospers because of his particular dishonesty, is the result of superficial judgment, which assumes that the dishonest man is almost totally corrupt, and the honest man almost entirely virtuous. In the light of a deeper knowledge and wider experience, such judgment is clearly erroneous. The dishonest man may have some admirable virtues the honest does not possess, and the honest man obnoxious vices absent in the dishonest. The honest man reaps the good results of his honest thoughts and acts ; he also brings upon himself the sufferings which his vices produce. The dishonest man likewise harvests his own suffering and happiness.

It is pleasing to human vanity to believe that we suffer because of our virtue. But not until a man has uprooted every sickly, bitter, and impure thought from his mind, and washed every sinful stain from his soul, can he be in a position to know and declare that his sufferings are the result of his good, and not of his bad qualities. Yet long before he has reached that supreme perfection he will have found, working in his mind and life, the great law of justice in which good cannot produce evil, nor evil good. Possessed of this knowledge, he then will know, looking back upon his past ignorance and blindness, that his life is, and always was, justly ordered, and that all his past experiences, good and bad, were the equitable working of his evolving, yet unevolved self.

Good thoughts and actions can never produce bad results; bad thoughts and actions can never produce good results. This is but saying that nothing can come from corn but corn, nothing from nettles but nettles.

Men understand this law in the natural world, and work with it; but few understand it in the mental and moral world (though its operation there is just as simple and undeviating), and they, therefore, do not co-operate with it.

Suffering is always the effect of wrong thought in some direction. It is an indication that the individual is out of harmony with himself, with the law of his being. The sole and supreme use of suffering is to purify, to burn out all that is useless and impure. Suffering ceases for him who is pure. There is no object in burning gold after the dross has been removed, and a perfectly pure and enlightened being does not suffer.

The circumstances which a man encounters with suffering are the result of his own mental inharmony. The circumstances which a man encounters with blessedness are the result of his own mental harmony. Blessedness, not material possessions, is the measure of right thought; wretchedness, not lack of material possessions, is the measure of wrong thought.

A man may be cursed and rich; he may be blessed and poor. Blessedness and riches are only joined together when the riches are rightly and wisely used, and the poor man only descends into wretchedness when he regards his lot as a burden unjustly imposed.

Indigence and overindulgence are the two extremes of wretchedness. They are both equally unnatural and the result of mental disorder. A man is not rightly conditioned until he is a happy, healthy, and prosperous being. Happiness, health, and prosperity are the result of a harmonious adjustment of the inner with the outer, of the man with his surroundings.

### ORGANIZE YOUR LIFE

A man only begins to be a man when he ceases to whine and revile, and commences to search for the hidden justice which regulates his life. And as he adapts his mind to that regulating factor, he ceases to accuse others of being the cause of his condition, and builds himself up in strong and noble thoughts. He ceases to kick against circumstances, but begins to use them as aids to his more rapid progress, and as a means of discovering the hidden powers and possibilities within himself.

Law, not confusion, is the dominating principle in the universe. Justice, not injustice, is the soul and substance of life. Righteousness, not corruption, is the molding and moving force in the spiritual government of the world. This being so, man has but to right himself to find that the universe is right. And during the process of putting himself right, he will find that as he alters his thoughts toward things, and other people, things and other people will alter toward him.

## THE EFFECTS OF BASE THOUGHTS

Men imagine that thought can be kept secret, but it cannot; it rapidly crystallizes into habit, and habit solidifies into circumstance:

¶ Bestial thoughts crystallize into habits of drunkenness and sensuality, which solidify into circumstances of destitution and disease.

¶ Impure thoughts of every kind crystallize into enervating and confusing habits, which solidify into distracting and adverse circumstances.

¶ Lazy thoughts crystallize into habits of uncleanliness and dishonesty, which solidify into circumstances of foulness and beggary.

¶ Hateful and condemnatory thoughts crystallize into habits of accusation and violence, which solidify into circumstances of injury and persecution.

¶ Selfish thoughts of all kinds crystallize into habits of self-seeking, which solidify into circumstances more or less distressing.

¶ Thoughts of fear, doubt, and indecision crystallize into weak, unmanly, and irresolute habits, which solidify into circumstances of failure, indigence, and slavish dependence.

### THE EFFECTS OF GOOD THOUGHTS

On the other hand, beautiful thoughts of all kinds crystallize into habits of grace and kindliness, which solidify into genial and sunny circumstances:

¶ Pure thoughts crystallize into habits of temperance and self-control, which solidify into circumstances of repose and peace.

¶ Energetic thoughts crystallize into habits of cleanliness and industry, which solidify into circumstances of pleasantness.

¶ Gentle and forgiving thoughts crystallize into habits of gentleness, which solidify into protective and preservative circumstances.

¶ Loving and unselfish thoughts crystallize into habits of self-forgetfulness for others, which solidify into circumstances of sure and abiding prosperity and true riches.

¶ Thoughts of courage, self-reliance, and decision crystallize into manly habits, which solidify into circumstances of success, plenty, and freedom.

"A strong body and a bright, happy or serene countenance can only result from the fine admittance of thoughts of joy and goodwill and serenity into the mind."

# Thoughts of Health

*It is part of the cure, to wish to be cured.*

SENECA

THE BODY is the servant of the mind. It obeys the operations of the mind, whether they are deliberately chosen or automatically expressed. At the bidding of unlawful thoughts the body sinks rapidly into disease and decay. At the command of glad and beautiful thoughts it becomes clothed with youthfulness and beauty.

Disease and health, like circumstances, are rooted in thought. Sickly thoughts will express themselves through a sickly body. Thoughts of fear have been known to kill a man as speedily as a bullet, and they are continually killing thousands of people just as surely though less rapidly. The people who live in fear of disease are the people who get it. Anxiety quickly demoralizes the whole body, and lays it open to the entrance of disease; while impure thoughts, even if not physically indulged, soon will shatter the nervous system.

Strong, pure, and happy thoughts build up the body in vigor and grace. The body is a delicate and plastic instrument, which responds readily to thought, and thought will produce its own effects, good or bad, upon it.

Man will continue to have impure and poisoned blood as long as he has unclean thoughts. Out of a clean heart comes a clean life and a clean body. Out of a defiled mind proceeds a defiled life and a corrupt body. Thought is the font of action, life, and manifestation; make the fountain pure, and all will be pure.

Change of diet will not help a man who will not change his thoughts. When a man makes his thoughts pure, he no longer desires impure food.

Clean thoughts make clean habits. The so-called saint who does not wash his body is not a saint. He who has strengthened and purified his thoughts does not need to consider the malevolent microbe.

### THE MIND CONTROLS HEALTH

If you would perfect your body, guard your mind. If you would renew your body, beautify your mind. Thoughts of malice, envy, disappointment, despondency, rob the body of its health and grace.

A sour face does not come by chance; it is made by sour thoughts. Wrinkles that mar are drawn by folly, passion, pride.

As you cannot have a sweet and wholesome home unless you admit the air and sunshine freely into your rooms, so a strong body and a bright, happy, or serene countenance can only result from the free admittance of thoughts of joy and good will and serenity into the mind.

On the faces of the aged there are wrinkles made by sympathy; others wrought by strong and pure thought, and others carved by passion. Who cannot distinguish them? With those who have lived righteously, age is calm, peaceful, and softly mellow, like the setting sun. I have recently seen a philosopher on his deathbed. He was not old except in years. He died as sweetly and peacefully as he had lived.

There is no physician like cheerful thought for dissipating the ills of the body; there is no comforter to compare with good will for dispersing the shadows of grief and sorrow. To live continually in thoughts of ill will, cynicism, suspicion, and envy, is to be confined in a self-made prison cell. But to think well of all, to be cheerful with all, to patiently learn to find good in all—such unselfish thoughts are the very portals of heaven.

# WORKING THOUGHTS

*Only begin and then the mind grows heated; only begin and the task will be completed.* GOETHE

"Aimlessness is a vice and such drifting must not continue for him who would steer clear of catastrophe and destruction."

UNTIL THOUGHT is linked with purpose there is no intelligent accomplishment. With the majority the ship of thought is allowed to "drift" upon the ocean of life. Aimlessness is a common vice, and such drifting must not continue for him who would steer clear of catastrophe and destruction.

They who have no central purpose in their life fall easy prey to petty worries, fears, troubles, and self-pityings, all of which are indications of weakness. All of which lead, just as surely as deliberately planned sins (though by a different route), to failure, unhappiness, and loss, for weakness cannot persist in a power-evolving universe.

A man should conceive of a legitimate purpose in his heart, and set out to accomplish it. He should make this purpose the centralizing point of his thoughts. It may take the form of a spiritual ideal, or it may be a worldly object, according to his nature at the time. But whichever it is, he should steadily focus his thought forces upon the object which he has set before him. He should make this purpose his supreme duty, and should devote himself to its attainment, not allowing his thoughts to wander away into short-lived fancies, longings, and imaginings. This is the royal road to self-control and true concentration of thought. Even if he fails again and again to accomplish his purpose (as he necessarily must until weakness is overcome), the strength of character gained will be the measure of his true success, and this will form a new starting point in his life for future power and triumph.

Those who are not prepared for the apprehension of a great purpose, should fix their thoughts upon the faultless performance of their duty, no matter how insignificant their task may appear. Only in this way can their thoughts be gathered and focused, and resolution and energy be developed. Being focused and developed, there is nothing which they may not accomplish.

### STRENGTH COMES WITH PURPOSE

The weakest soul, knowing its own weakness, and believing this truth—that strength can only be developed by effort and practice—will, thus believing, at once begin to exert itself. And by adding effort to effort, patience to patience, and strength to strength, it will never cease to develop, and will at last grow divinely strong.

As the physically weak man can make himself strong by careful and patient training, so the weak thinking man can make himself strong by exercising himself in right thinking.

To put away aimlessness and weakness, and to begin to think with purpose, is to enter the ranks of those strong ones who only recognize failure as one of the pathways to attainment; who make all conditions serve them, and who think strongly, attempt fearlessly, and accomplish masterfully.

Having conceived of his purpose, a man should mentally mark out a straight pathway to its achievement, looking neither to the right nor the left. Doubts and fears should be rigorously excluded. They are disintegrating elements which break up the straight line of effort, rendering it crooked, ineffectual, useless. Thoughts of doubt and fear never accomplish anything, and never can. They always lead to failure. Purpose, energy, power to do, and all strong thoughts cease when doubt and fear creep in.

### ELIMINATE THE NEGATIVE

The will to do springs from the knowledge that we can do. Doubt and fear are the great enemies of knowledge, and he who encourages them, who does not slay them, thwarts himself at every step.

He who has conquered doubt and fear has conquered failure. His every thought is allied with power, and all difficulties are bravely met and wisely overcome. His purposes are seasonably planted, and they bloom and bring forth fruit which does not fall prematurely to the ground.

Thought allied fearlessly to purpose becomes

creative force. He who knows this is ready to become something higher and stronger than a mere bundle of wavering thoughts and fluctuating sensations. He who does this has become the conscious and intelligent wielder of his mental powers.

"A man can only rise,
conquer and achieve by
lifting up his thoughts."

# THINKING OF SUCCESS

*Assume a virtue though you have it not.*

WILLIAM SHAKESPEARE

ALL THAT a man achieves and all that he fails to achieve is the direct result of his own thoughts. In a justly ordered universe, individual responsibility must be absolute. A man's weakness and strength, purity and impurity, are his own, and not another man's. They are brought about by himself, and not by another. They can only be altered by himself, never by another. His condition also is his own. His suffering and his happiness are evolved from within. As he thinks, so he is; as he continues to think, so he remains.

A strong man cannot help a weaker unless that weaker is willing to be helped, and even then the weak man must become strong of himself. He must, by his own efforts, develop the strength which he admires in another. None but himself can alter his condition.

It has been usual for men to think and to say, "Many men are slaves because one is an oppressor; let us hate the oppressor." Now, however, there is an increasing tendency to reverse this judgment, and to say, "One man is an oppressor because many are slaves; let us despise the slaves."

The truth is that oppressor and slave are co-operators in ignorance, and, while seeming to afflict each other, are in reality afflicting themselves. A perfect knowledge perceives the weakness of the oppressed and the misapplied power of the oppressor. A perfect love sees the suffering which each entails and condemns neither. A perfect compassion embraces oppressor and oppressed.

He who has conquered weakness, and has put away all selfish thoughts, belongs neither to oppressor nor oppressed. He is free.

A man can only rise, conquer, and achieve by lifting up his thoughts. He can only remain weak, and abject, and miserable by refusing to lift up his thoughts.

### ELEVATE YOUR THOUGHTS

Before a man can achieve anything, even in worldly things, he must lift his thoughts above slavish animal indulgence. He may not, in order to succeed, necessarily give up all animality and selfishness, by any means. But he must sacrifice a large part of it.

A man whose first thought is bestial indulgence could neither think clearly nor plan methodically; he could not find and develop his latent resources, and would fail in any undertaking. Not having commenced manfully to control his thoughts, he is not in a position to control affairs and to adopt serious responsibilities. He is not fit to act independently and stand alone. But he is limited, however, only by the thoughts which he chooses.

There can be no progress, no achievement, without sacrifice. A man's worldly success will occur in the measure that he sacrifices his confused animal thoughts, and fixes his mind on the development of his plans, and the strengthening of his resolution and self-reliance. And the higher he lifts his thoughts, the more manly, upright, and righteous he will become, the greater will be his success, and the more blessed and enduring will be his achievements.

The universe does not favor the greedy, the dishonest, the vicious, although on the surface it may sometimes appear to do so. It helps the honest, the magnanimous, the virtuous. All the great Teachers of the ages have declared this in varying forms, and to prove and know it a man has but to persist in making himself more and more virtuous by lifting up his thoughts.

### STRENGTHEN YOUR SPIRIT

Spiritual achievements are the consummation of holy aspirations. He who lives constantly in the conception of noble and lofty thoughts, who dwells upon all that is pure and unselfish, will, as surely as the sun reaches its zenith and the moon its full, become wise and noble in character, and rise into a position of influence and blessedness.

Achievement, of whatever kind, is the crown of effort, the diadem of thought. By the aid of self-control, resolution, purity, righteousness, and well-directed thought a man ascends. By the aid of animality, indolence, impurity, corruption, and confusion of thought a man descends.

A man who has risen to the heights of success in the world, and even to lofty altitudes in the spiritual realm, may descend into weakness and wretchedness by allowing arrogant, selfish, and corrupt thoughts to take possession of him.

Victories attained by right thought can only be maintained by watchfulness. Many give way when success is assured, and rapidly fall back into failure.

All achievements, whether in the business, intellectual, or spiritual world, are the result of definitely directed thought, are governed by the same law, and are of the same method. The only difference lies in the object of attainment.

He who would accomplish little need sacrifice little, but he who would achieve much must sacrifice much.

# VISIONS AND IDEALS

*A wise man will make more opportunities than he finds.* FRANCIS BACON

"The greatest achievements were at first and for a time dreams; the great oak sleeps in the acorn."

THE DREAMERS are the saviors of the world. As the visible world is sustained by the invisible, so men, through all their trials and sins and sordid vocations, are nourished by the beautiful visions of their individual dreamers.

Humanity cannot forget its dreamers; it cannot let their ideals fade and die; it lives in them; it knows them as the realities which it shall one day see and know.

Composer, sculptor, painter, poet, prophet, and sage, these are the makers of the afterworld, the architects of heaven. The world is beautiful because they have lived; without them, laboring humanity would perish.

He who cherishes a beautiful vision, a lofty ideal in his heart, will one day realize it.

Columbus cherished a vision of another world, and he discovered it.

Copernicus fostered the vision of a multiplicity of worlds, and he revealed it.

Gautama Buddha beheld the vision of a spiritual world of stainless beauty and perfect peace, and he entered into it.

Cherish your visions; cherish your ideals; cherish the music that stirs in your heart, the beauty that forms in your mind, the loveliness that drapes your purest thoughts. Out of them will grow all delightful conditions, all heavenly environment.

Of them, if you but remain true to them, your world will at last be built.

To desire is to obtain; to aspire is to achieve. Shall man's basest desires receive the fullest measure of gratification, and his purest aspirations starve for lack of sustenance? Such is not the law. Such a condition of things can never be.

Dream lofty dreams, and as you dream, so shall you become. Your vision is the promise of what you shall one day be; your ideal is the prophecy of what you shall at last unveil.

## LOOK INWARD FOR INSPIRATION

The greatest achievements were at first and for a time dreams. The oak sleeps in the acorn; the bird waits in the egg, and a waking angel stirs in the highest vision of the soul. Dreams are the seedlings of realities.

Your circumstances may be uncongenial, but they shall not long remain so if you but perceive an ideal and strive to reach it. You cannot travel within and stand still without.

Here is a youth hard pressed by poverty and labor; confined long hours in an unhealthy workshop; unschooled, and lacking all the arts of refinement. But he dreams of better things. He thinks of intelligence, of refinement, of grace and beauty. He conceives of and mentally builds up an ideal condition of life. The vision of a wider liberty and a larger scope takes possession of him. Unrest urges him to action, and he utilizes all his spare time and means to the development of his latent powers and resources.

Very soon so altered has his mind become that the workshop can no longer hold him. It has become so out of harmony with his mentality that it falls out of his life as a garment is cast aside, and, with the growth of opportunities which fit the scope of his expanding powers, he passes out of it forever.

### A MASTER OF FORCES

Years later we see this youth as a full-grown man. We find him a master of certain forces of the mind which he wields with world-wide influence and almost unequaled power. In his hands he holds the cords of gigantic responsibilities. He speaks, and lives are changed; men and women hang upon his words and thoughts and remold their characters, sunlike, he becomes the fixed and luminous center around which innumerable destinies revolve.

He has realized the vision of his youth. He has become one with his ideal. And you, too, will realize the vision (not the idle wish) of your heart, be it base or beautiful, or a mixture of the two, for you will always gravitate toward that which you most love. In your hands will be placed the exact results of your own thoughts; you will receive what you earn; no more, no less. Whatever your present environment may be, you will fall, remain, or rise with your thoughts, your vision, your ideal.

### THE POWER OF AN IDEA

You will become as small as your controlling desire; as great as your dominant aspiration. In the words of Stanton Kirkham Davis, "You may be keeping accounts, and presently you shall walk out the door that for so long has seemed to you the barrier of your ideals, and shall find yourself before an audience—the pen still behind your ear, the ink stains on your fingers—and then and there shall pour out the torrent of your inspiration. You may be driving sheep, and you shall wander to the city—innocent and openmouthed; you shall wander under the bold guidance of the spirit into the studio of the master, and after a time he shall say, 'I have nothing more to teach you.' And now you have become the master, who did so recently dream of great things while driving sheep. You shall lay down your staff to take upon yourself the regeneration of the world.''

### LUCK IS A MISNOMER

The thoughtless, the ignorant, and the indolent, seeing only the apparent effects of things and not the things themselves, talk of luck, of fortune, and chance. Seeing a man grow rich, they say, ''How lucky he is!'' Observing another become intellectual, they exclaim, ''How highly favored he is!'' And noting the saintly character and wide influence of another, they remark, ''How chance aids him at every turn!''

They do not see the trials and failures and struggles which these men have voluntarily encountered in order to gain their experience. They have no knowledge of the sacrifices these men have made, of the undaunted efforts they have put forth, of the faith they have exercised, that they might overcome the apparently insurmountable, and realize the vision of their hearts.

They do not know the darkness and the heart-aches; they only see the light and joy, and call it "luck." They do not see the long and arduous journey, but only behold the pleasant goal, and call it "good fortune." They do not understand the process, but only perceive the result, and call it "chance."

In all human affairs there are efforts, and there are results, and the strength of the effort is the measure of the result. Chance is not. Gifts; powers; material, intellectual, and spiritual possessions, are the fruits of effort; they are thoughts completed, objects accomplished, visions realized.

The vision that you glorify in your mind, the ideal that you enthrone in your heart—this you will build your life by, this you will become.

"In the ocean of life the isles of blessedness are awaiting and the sunny shore of your ideals awaits your coming."

# Peace of Mind

*Nothing can bring you peace but yourself.*     RALPH WALDO EMERSON

CALMNESS of mind is one of the beautiful jewels of wisdom. It is the result of long and patient effort in self-control. Its presence is an indication of ripened experience, and of a more than ordinary knowledge of the laws and operations of thought.

A man becomes calm in the measure that he understands himself as a thought-evolved being. This knowledge necessitates the understanding of others as the result of thought. And as he develops a right understanding, and sees more and more clearly the internal relations of things by the action of cause and effect, he ceases to fuss and fume and worry and grieve, and remains poised, steadfast, and serene.

The happy man, having learned how to govern himself, knows how to adapt himself to others; and they, in turn, revere his spiritual strength, and feel that they can learn of him and rely upon him. The more tranquil a man becomes, the greater is his success, his influence, his power for good. Even the ordinary businessman finds his business prosperity increases as he develops a greater self-control and equanimity. For people always prefer to deal with a man whose behavior is equable.

The strong, calm man is always loved and revered. He is like a shade-giving tree in a thirsty land, or a sheltering rock in a storm. Who does not love a tranquil heart, a sweet-tempered, balanced disposition? It does not matter whether it rains or shines, or what changes come to those possessing these blessings, for they are always sweet, serene, and calm.

That exquisite poise of character which we call serenity is the final lesson of culture; it is the flowering of life, the fruit of the soul. It is as precious as wisdom, more to be desired than gold —yes, even than fine gold.

How insignificant money-seeking looks in comparison with a happy life—a life that dwells in the ocean of truth, beneath the waves, beyond the reach of tempests, in the eternal calm!

How many people we know who sour their lives, who destroy their poise of character, who ruin all that is sweet and beautiful by explosive tempers! It is a question of whether or not the great majority of people do not ruin their lives and mar their happiness by lack of self-control. How few people we meet in life who are well-balanced, who have that exquisite poise which is characteristic of the finished character!

Yes, humanity surges with uncontrolled passion, is tumultuous with ungoverned grief, is blown about by anxiety and doubt. Only the wise man, only he whose thoughts are controlled and purified, makes the winds and storms of the soul obey him.

Tempest-tossed souls, wherever you may be, under whatsoever conditions you may live, know this—in the ocean of life the isles of blessedness are smiling, and the sunny shore of your ideal awaits your coming. Keep your hand firmly upon the helm of thought. In the ship of your soul reclines the commanding master. He does but sleep; wake him.

Set in Monotype Perpetua,
a classic type-face designed in 1922
by Eric Gill, sculptor and engraver.
Printed on Hallmark Eggshell Book paper.
Designed by J. William Burdett.